Josef Polleross

Heute

Jüdisches Leben in Wien
Jewish Life in Vienna

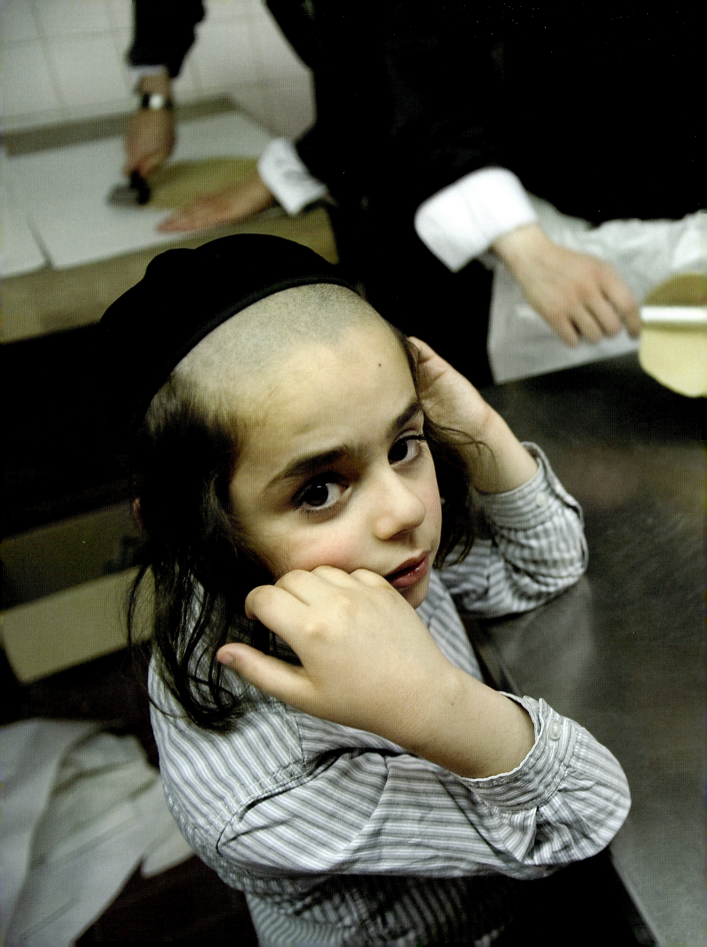

Josef Polleross

Heute

Jüdisches Leben in Wien
Jewish Life in Vienna

Metroverlag

Inhalt Contents

Glaube Faith — 11

Alltag Daily Life — 45

Bildung & Sport Education & Sport — 71

Kultur Culture — 87

Gestern Yesterday — 115

Feste Feasts — 135

Heute in Wien

„Heute" ist mehr als eine Momentaufnahme aktuellen jüdischen Lebens in Wien. Dem Fotografen Josef Polleross ist es gelungen, jenseits der spannenden Welt der Reportagefotografie, aus der er kommt, den Zustand der Wiener jüdischen Gemeinde im Detail zu erfassen. Einer Gemeinde, die trotz ihrer zahlenmäßigen Begrenztheit lebendig und facettenreich ist wie kaum eine andere.

Polleross bietet nicht nur durch beeindruckende Porträts Einblicke in das gegenwärtige jüdische Gemeindeleben. Er hat über viele Monate hinweg Feiern und Feiertage, jüdische Organisationen, Schulen, Kinder- und Jugendclubs, Seniorentreffpunkte, Veranstaltungen, kulturelle Ereignisse, ja nahezu alles, was sich heute in der sogenannten jüdischen Gasse ereignet, besucht und fotografisch dokumentiert. „Heute" zeigt eine selbstbewusste jüdische Gemeinde, deren Mitglieder längst nicht mehr auf ihren gepackten Koffern sitzen oder sie für den Notfall bereithalten. Eine Gemeinde, die hauptsächlich aus Juden besteht, die in erster, zweiter und mittlerweile dritter und vierter Generation in Wien leben.

Nach der Shoah hatte die Mehrheit der jüdischen Familien in Wien keine Wurzeln in dieser Stadt. Sie stammten aus Galizien, Ungarn, Polen oder Rumänien. Als Überlebende waren sie nach dem Ende des Zweiten Weltkriegs sogenannte Displaced Persons, Menschen ohne Heimat, ohne Familie, die durch Zufall in Wien gelandet sind. Die meisten hatten viele oder alle Verwandten verloren. Wien wurde für sie zum neuen Lebensmittelpunkt. Viele fanden hier neue Lebenspartner, gründeten eine Familie und bauten eine berufliche Existenz auf.

Es ist auch die neuere Generation an Zuwanderern, die Josef Polleross bei seinen Spaziergängen durch das „Jüdische Wien heute" fotografisch eingefangen hat, vor allem aus der ehemaligen Sowjetunion. Aschkenasische Juden mit europäischen Wurzeln oder sephardische Juden aus Regionen wie Usbekistan, Tadschikistan, Georgien oder Aserbaidschan. Alle haben ihren eigenen kulturellen Hintergrund und ihre eigene Mentalität hierher mitgebracht. Manchmal kommen viele dieser Gruppen zusammen, um Feiertage oder festliche Ereignisse zu begehen.

Ein Höhepunkt dieses neuen jüdischen Bewusstseins in Wien waren die Maccabi Games, die jüdische Olympiade, die 2011 in Wien stattfand. Das Wiener Rathaus war mit der israelischen Fahne beflaggt, 2.000 jüdische Sportler aus aller Welt zogen daran vorbei. Ein Meilenstein in der jüdischen Nachkriegsgeschichte Wiens und damit ein essenzieller Punkt in der Dokumentation von Josef Polleross.

Mit Josef Polleross hat mich mein ehemaliger ORF-Kollege, der Nahost-Korrespondent Karim El-Gawhary, bekannt gemacht. Polleross hat bereits in den verschiedensten Weltgegenden gelebt und gearbeitet, so auch in Kairo als Fotograf u. a. für die New York Times. Zu diesem Zeitpunkt fotografierte Polleross Vertretungen der Chabad-Bewegungen, und wir kamen ins Gespräch. Er erzählte mir, dass es ihm ein großes Anliegen sei, die jüdische Gemeinde Wiens neu zu dokumentieren. Ein Ansinnen, dem ich vorerst etwas skeptisch gegenüberstand. Schnell wurde ich von der Qualität seiner Arbeit, aber auch von seinem tiefen Engagement überzeugt. Vor allem erinnerte mich seine Herangehensweise an das Projekt des Fotografen Harry Weber, dessen Idee wir mit dieser Serie fortsetzen.

Die Ausstellung und das Buch von Harry Weber aus dem Jahr 1996 bleiben mir unauslöschlich in Erinnerung. Der unvergessliche Wiener Fotograf Weber (1921–2007) hat Anfang der 1990er-Jahre fotografische Streifzüge durch die Wiener jüdische Gemeinde unternommen. Das „heutige jüdische Leben" mit der Kamera festzuhalten, war sein Ziel. Er traf eine sehr subjektive Auswahl: Er fotografierte, was ihn am Alltag der Juden in Wien interessierte und wovon er glaubte, es sei wichtig, um ein Porträt der vielschichtigen jüdischen Gegenwart zu zeichnen.

So kam Harry Weber auch auf mich und ich zu ihm. In seiner Sammlung an Sujets fehlte ihm damals eine jüdische Hochzeit. Harry Weber hatte erfahren, dass meine Hochzeit kurz bevorstand. Eine Ablehnung seines Ansinnens kam für ihn nicht infrage. Auch nicht, als mein künftiger Ehemann Martin Engelberg und ich ihm erklärten, dass wir in einer kleinen Runde in Israel heiraten wollten. Harry war hartnäckig. Er fuhr mit uns nach Eilat und fotografierte unseren Polterabend, unsere Hochzeit, die Schewa Brachot, und es entstand mit vielen unserer Freunde eine enge Beziehung. Es war der Beginn einer Freundschaft, Harry Weber begleitete Martin und mich durch unsere nächsten wichtigen emotionalen Lebensabschnitte. Die Geburt unseres Sohnes, die Brit Mila etc. Kurz vor der Bar Mitzwa unseres Sohnes ist Harry leider von dieser Welt gegangen. Wir vermissen ihn sehr.

Harry Webers damalige Streifzüge dokumentieren ein Stück Wiener jüdische Geschichte. Unser Sohn, unsere Töchter wachsen heran. Heute in Wien. Das ist nicht mehr das Heute, das Harry Weber vor bald 20 Jahren eingefangen hat. Viel hat sich bewegt, verändert, manches ist gleich geblieben.

Die jüdische Gegenwart in Wien. Oft habe ich mich gefragt, ob und wie sich die Bilderreise von Harry Weber fortsetzen ließe. Als dann eines Tages durch Zufall Josef Polleross in mein Leben trat, begann eine Zeitreise. Sein Portfolio überzeugte mich, und so können wir uns heute glücklich schätzen, eine weitere wichtige Etappe des jüdischen Lebens in Wien nicht nur dokumentiert zu wissen, sondern durch Josef Polleross auch wunderbar künstlerisch festgehalten zu haben. Ich danke ihm, aber auch Dr. Astrid Peterle, die die Ausstellung im Museum Judenplatz kuratorisch begleitet hat, von Herzen.

Zu Pessach lesen wir den Auszug aus Ägypten, die Haggada. Darin steht geschrieben, dass man dieses Ereignis seinen Kindern weitererzählen soll. „Ledor vador" – von Generation zu Generation sollen jüdische Erfahrungen weitergegeben werden, um den Glauben und die Tradition zu bewahren. Diese Fotodokumentation jüdischen Lebens trägt auch dazu bei, die Erfahrung und die Stimmung einzufangen und damit weiterzugeben.

Danielle Spera

Today in Vienna

"Today in Vienna" is more than a snapshot of the current Jewish life in Vienna. Beyond the exciting world of photojournalism, the photographer Josef Polleross successfully and elaborately captured the situation of the Jewish community in Vienna. A community that is vital and multifaceted unlike hardly any other despite its comparatively small membership.

Polleross offers insights into the current Jewish community life not only by taking impressive portraits. For several months, he has visited and photographed Jewish ceremonies and holidays, Jewish organizations, schools, children's and youth clubs, senior associations, cultural and other events – almost everything that happens today on the so-called Jewish street. "Today in Vienna – 2012" shows a confident Jewish community whose members have long ago abandoned to sit on their packed suitcases or keep them ready just in case. The members of this community are mainly Jews who are first or second generation or by now even third or fourth generation in Vienna.

After the Shoah, the majority of the Jewish families in Vienna did not have any roots in this city. They came from Galicia, Hungary, Poland or Rumania. Having survived the Second World War, they were called displaced persons, people without home, without family, who came to Vienna by coincidence. Most of them had lost many or all of their relatives. Vienna became their new center of life. Many of them found new partners here, started a family and established a professional existence.

It is also the newer generation of immigrants who mainly come from the former Soviet Union who Josef Polleross photographed during his walks through today's Jewish Vienna. Ashkenazic Jews with European roots or Sephardic Jews from regions like Uzbekistan, Tajikistan, Georgia or Azerbaijan. All of them have brought along their own cultural background and their own mentality. From time to time, these groups come together to celebrate holidays or festive events.

A highlight of this new Jewish identity in Vienna were the Maccabi Games, the Jewish Olympics, which were held in Vienna in 2011. The flag of Israel was shown on the Vienna City Hall where 2,000 Jewish athletes from all over the world passed by. A milestone in the Jewish post-war history of Vienna and therefore an essential part of Josef Polleross's documentation.

It was Karim El-Gawhary, one of my former colleagues, who worked as Middle East correspondent at the Austrian broadcasting company ORF who introduced me to Josef Polleross. Polleross has lived and worked in the most different parts of the world as for example in Cairo where he worked amongst others as a photographer for the New York Times. When we met, Polleross was photographing representatives of the Chabad movement and we got into conversation. He told me that he wished to document the Jewish community in Vienna in a new way. At that moment, I had my reservations about his request. But soon the quality of his work convinced me of his true commitment. His approach particularly reminded me of the project of the photographer Harry Weber whose idea we continued with this series.

Harry Weber's exhibition and book from 1996 will remain imprinted in my memory. At the beginning of the 1990ies, the unforgettable Viennese photographer Weber (1921-2007) went on photographic rambles in the Jewish community of Vienna. His aim was to capture "today's Jewish life" with his camera. His selection was very subjective: He photographed everything in which he was interested in the everyday life of the Viennese Jews and which he thought would be important to draw a portrait of the complex Jewish present. In this context, I got to know Harry Weber. Back then, his collection of subjects lacked a Jewish wedding.

Harry Weber had heard that my wedding was coming up. For him, refusing his request was beyond debate. Not even after my future husband Martin Engelberg and I told him that we wanted to get married in an intimate circle in Israel. Harry persisted. He went with us to Eilat and photographed our wedding eve party, our wedding, the Sheva Brachot and developed close relations with many of our friends. This was the beginning of a friendship and Harry Weber accompanied Martin and me through further important emotional periods of our life like the birth of our son, Brit Milah, etc. Unfortunately, just before our son's Bar Mitzvah, Harry deceased. We miss him a lot.

Harry Weber's then photographic rambles documented a part of the Jewish history in Vienna. Our son, our daughters are growing up. Today in Vienna. It is no longer the present that Harry Weber caught almost 20 years ago. Many things have moved, changed, some have remained the same.

The Jewish present in Vienna. I often asked myself if and how Harry Weber's photographic travel could be continued. And then I met Josef Polleross by coincidence and the time travel began. His portfolio convinced me and today we can consider ourselves happy that Josef Polleross has not only documented but also artistically recorded another important stage of Jewish life in Vienna. I would like to thank him and also Dr. Astrid Peterle, the curator of the exhibition at the Museum Judenplatz.

At Passover, we read the Exodus from Egypt, the Haggadah. According to it, we shall tell our children about this event. "Ledor vador" – from generation to generation, we shall pass on the Jewish experience to preserve our faith and tradition. This photographic documentary of Jewish life contributes to catch the experience and atmosphere and to pass them on to our children.

Danielle Spera

Faith
Glaube

Seiten 10/11:
Stadttempel: Oberrabbiner Paul Chaim Eisenberg ist Gastgeber des „Großen Kantorenkonzerts". Oberkantor Zvi Weiss (Israel), Oberkantor Benjamin Muller (Antwerpen) und am Klavier Menachem Bristowski (Israel).

Pages 10/11:
Central City Temple: Chief Rabbi Paul Chaim Eisenberg is the host of "Big Cantor Concert". Chief Cantor Zvi Weiss (Israel), Chief Cantor Benjamin Muller (Antwerp) and on the piano Menachem Bristowski (Israel).

Stadttempel: Morgengebet
Central City Temple: morning prayer

Professor Rosenkranz zeigt kanadischen Studenten den Stadttempel.
Prof. Rosenkranz is showing the Central City Temple to Canadian students.

Israelische Kultusgemeinde Wien (IKG): Oberkantor Shmuel Barzilai übt für die Bar Mitzwa mit Nathaniel.
Jewish Community Vienna: Cantor Shmuel Barzilai practices with Nathaniel for his Bar Mitzvah.

Israelische Kultusgemeinde Wien (IKG), Wiener jüdisches Archiv: Geburts-, Heirats- und Sterbematriken der jüdischen Gemeinschaft 1826–1938 für öffentliche und private Nachforschungen. Wolf-Erich Eckstein ist der Leiter.
Jewish Community Vienna, Vienna Jewish Records Office: Birth-, marriage- and death records of the Jewish Community 1826 – 1938, available for public and private research. Wolf-Erich Eckstein is in charge.

Brit Mila
Brit Milah

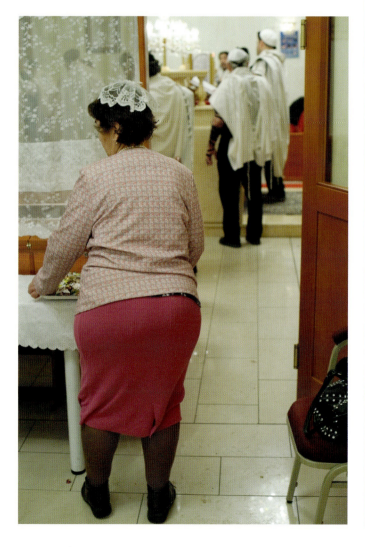

Synagoge Blumauergasse: Bar Mitzwa
Synagogue Blumauergasse: Bar Mitzvah

Sefardisches Zentrum – Bucharische Synagoge: Bar Mitzwa
Sephardic Centre – Bukhara Synagogue: Bar Mitzvah

Beit Halevi: Bar Mitzwa
Beit Halevi: Bar Mitzvah

Sefardisches Zentrum – Bucharische Synagoge: Bar Mitzwa
Sephardic Centre – Bukhara Synagogue: Bar Mitzvah

Mikwe Große Mohrengasse
Mikveh Grosse Mohrengasse

Zwi Perez Chajes Schule: Morgengebet in der Schul-Synagoge
Zwi Perez Chajes School: Morning prayer at the school's synagogue

Chanukka-Fest in der Wiener Jeschiwah
Hanukkah celebration at the Viennese Yeshiva

Agudas Jeschurun Synagoge
Agudas Jeschurun Synagogue

Wiener Jeschiwah: Rabbiner Weiss interpretiert Bibeltexte.
Viennese Yeshiva: Rabbi Weiss interpreting holy scriptures.

Khal Chassidim Synagoge
Khal Chassidim Synagogue

Seiten 32/33:
Ohel Moshe Synagoge:
Wiener Akademie für
Höhere Rabbinische
Studien
Pages 32/33:
Ohel Moshe Synagogue:
Vienna Academy of Higher
Rabbinical Studies

Ohel Moshe Synagoge:
Nesanel Lev ist Experte für
alte hebräische Schriften.
Ohel Moshe Synagogue:
Nesanel Lev is an expert for
ancient Hebrew scriptures.

Or Chadasch: Bibeltext-Analyse
Or Chadasch: bible study

Mesusot wird von Herrn Kohn überprüft.
Mezuzot is checked by Mr. Kohn.

Rosch ha-Schana (jüdischer Neujahrstag): das symbolische Wegwerfen von Sünden ins Wasser.
Rosh Hashanah (Jewish New Year): the ritual of tashlikh – one's sins are symbolically cast into the water.

Sefardisches Zentrum: Morgengebet in der Georgischen Synagoge
Sephardic Centre: morning prayer at the Georgian Synagogue

Jeden Freitag besucht Chabad-Rabbiner Benjamin Sufiev Juden aus Osteuropa in ihren Geschäften, um ihnen zu zeigen, wie man eine Tefillin anbringt und die dazugehörigen Gebete spricht.
Every Friday Chabad Rabbi Benjamin Sufiev visits jews from Eastern Europe at their shops to teach them how to put on tefillin and say the appropriate prayers.

Hochzeitsfeier
Wedding

Hochzeitsfeiern
Weddings

Hochzeit im Kursalon Hübner
Wedding at Kursalon Hübner

Alltag Daily Life

Seiten 44/45:
Koscherer Supermarkt
Padani
Pages 44/45:
Kosher supermarket Padani

Koscheres Fischgeschäft
„Fische & mehr KG"
Kosher fish store "Fische &
mehr KG"

Koschere Bäckerei Chaj
Kosher bakery Chaj

Koscherer Fleischhauer Bahur Tov
Kosher butcher Bahur Tov

Rund um den Karmelitermarkt
Karmelitermarkt neighbourhood

Obst & Gemüse Niyazov
Grocery store Niyazov

Kosherland Supermarkt
Kosherland supermarket

Ohel Moshe koschere Bäckerei
Ohel Moshe kosher bakery

Pain au Chocolat: Schneor Zivions Schokolade- und Patisserie-Produktion
Pain au Chocolat: Schneor Zivion's pastry and chocolate production

Herr Kohn hilft Rabbiner Hofmeister beim Keltern von Trauben.
Rabbi Hofmeister is making wine with the help of Mr. Kohn.

Restaurant Neni: die Familie Molcho
Restaurant Neni: the Molcho family

Maimonides Zentrum: Koscheres Essen wird für „Essen auf Rädern" verpackt.
Maimonides Centre: Taping the kosher food for delivery to hospitals and elderly people.

Das italienische Restaurant Novellino serviert koscheres Essen.
The Italian restaurant Novellino serves kosher food.

Restaurant Buchara Palace: Yahrzeit (Familie bei der Gedenkfeier am 8. Todestag des Familienoberhauptes)
Restaurant Buchara Palace: The annual anniversary of the death of a person is called the Yahrzeit. 8 year anniversary of the patriarch of the family.

Taborstraße: die koschere Pizzeria Prego
Taborstrasse: the kosher Pizza restaurant Prego

Der koschere Fleischhauer Ainhorn. Eine Wiener Tradition: Schawarma wird am Tag vor Pessach gegessen.
The kosher butcher Ainhorn. A local tradition in Vienna: Shawarma is served on the day before Pesach.

Koscheres Restaurant Simchas: Der Besitzer Herr Simchas sitzt rechts.
Kosher Restaurant Simchas: the owner is Mr. Simchas on the right side.

Prof. Rosenkranz mit Freunden bei der Aida Rotenturmstraße
Prof. Rosenkranz with friends at Aida Rotenturmstrasse

Gebet am Wiener Flughafen
Praying at the Vienna airport

Böcklinstraße: beim Fahrradhändler
Böcklinstraße: at the bike shop

Maimonides Zentrum:
Anne Kohn-Feuermann-
Tagesstätte
Maimonides Centre:
Anne Kohn-Feuermann-
Daycare Centre

Centropa Chanukka-Feier im Gemeindezentrum der IKG
(Israelitische Kultusgemeinde)
Centropa Hanukkah celebration at the Jewish Community Centre

Lilli und Max Tauber in ihrer Wohnung
Lilli and Max Tauber in their apartment

Maimonides Zentrum: Sabbat-Feier
Maimonides Centre: Shabbat dinner

Maimonides Zentrum
Maimonides Centre

Hansi Tausig organisiert Museumsbesuche für die ältere Generation.
Hansi Tausig is organizing museum visits for the older generation.

Das psychosoziale Zentrum ESRA (Hebräisch für „Hilfe") wurde 1994 in erster Linie als Beratungs- und Behandlungszentrum für Überlebende des Holocaust und deren Angehörige gegründet.
Club Schelanu: Zeichnen für ältere Menschen.
ESRA (Hebrew for 'help') was established in 1994 to provide medical, therapeutic and social work services to Holocaust survivors and their families.
Club Schelanu: Drawing for older people.

Club Schelanu im Beratungs- und Behandlungszentrum ESRA: Tanzen für ältere Menschen.
Club Schelanu at the ESRA-Centre: Dancing for older people.

Jüdischer Friedhof Seegasse
Jewish Cemetery Seegasse

Döblinger Friedhof: ehemaliger jüdischer Friedhof –
das ehemalige Grab von Theodor Herzl
*Cemetery Döbling: former Jewish Cemetery –
where Theodor Herzl was buried*

Währinger Friedhof
Cemetery Währing

Education
Bildung & Sport

Seiten 70/71: Lauder Chabad Schule: Rabbiner Schmuel Alperovits mit Schülern. Flaktürme im Augarten aus der NS-Zeit im Hintergrund.
Pages 70/71: Lauder Chabad School: Rabbi Schmuel Alperovits with students. Antiaircraft gun towers built by the Nazis in the background.

Lauder Chabad Schule
Lauder Chabad School

Zwi Peres Chajes Schule (ZPC): Hebräische Klasse mit Tanz, Malerei und Schauspielerei
Zwi Perez Chajes School (ZPC): special Hebrew class with dance, painting and performances

Zwi Peres Chajes Schule
Zwi Perez Chajes School

Agudas Israel: Kindergarten, Volksschule, Mittelschule für Knaben und Mädchen
Agudas Israel: kindergarten, primary school and junior high school for boys and girls

Modeschau im Jüdischen Beruflichen Bildungszentrum (JBBZ)
Fashion show at the Jewish Vocational Educational Centre

JBBZ: Jüdisches Berufliches Bildungszentrum – IT-Technik-Ausbildung
Jewish Vocational Educational Centre: training to become a Computer technician

Jehuda Halevi Musikschule: Geigenunterricht
Jehuda Halevi Music School: violin lessons

Jehuda Halevi Musikschule: Chorunterricht
Jehuda Halevi Music School: choir lessons

Jüdisches Institut für Erwachsenenbildung: Hava Nagila Tanzgruppe
Jewish Institute for Adult Education: Hava Nagila dance troupe

Lauder Business School: Abschlussfeier
Lauder Business School: Graduation ceremony

Die Jugendorganisation
Bnei Akiva
*At the youth organization
Bnei Akiva*

US-Frauen-Fußballteam
US women's soccer team

Europäische Makkabi-Spiele 2011
European Maccabi Games 2011

Europäische Makkabi-Spiele 2011:
Eröffnungsfeier beim Rathaus
*European Maccabi Games 2011:
opening ceremony at city hall*

Vienna-Capitals-Eishockey-Spieler Raphael Rotter gibt ein Autogramm.
Vienna Capitals ice hockey player Raphael Rotter is autographing a shirt.

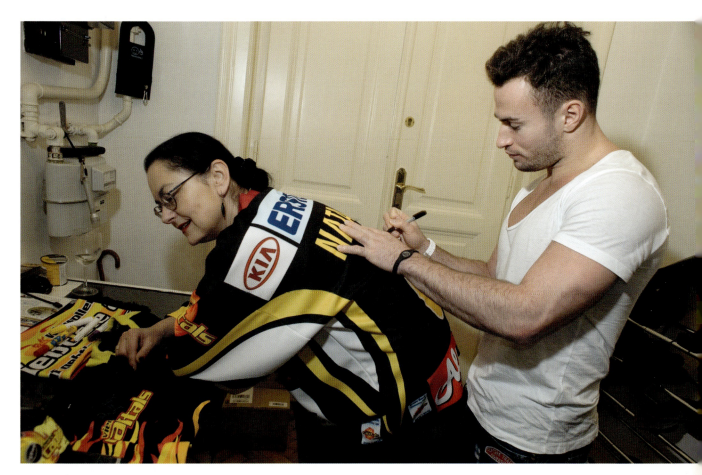

SC Maccabi Wien Fußballverein
SC Maccabi Vienna soccer club

Hakoah-Ringtrainer Anatoli Khalkadarov
Hakoah wrestling trainer Anatoli Khalkadarov

Sport Club Hakoah: Judo-Kurs
Sport Club Hakoah: Judo lessons

Culture
Kultur

Seiten 86–88:
Sigmund-Freud-Haus und
-Museum, Berggasse 19
Pages 86–88:
Sigmund Freud House and
Museum, Berggasse 19

Seiten 89/90: Jüdischer Chor Wien: Chorleiter Roman Grinberg während der Probe
Pages 89/90: Jewish Choir Vienna: conductor Roman Grinberg leading a weekly choir practice session

Anna Sushon: Dirigentin, Korrepetitorin
Anna Sushon: conductor and répétiteur (vocal coach)

Vien – mayn shtot

Vien iz di shtot, vu in vals men zikh dreyt,
Vien iz tsum tantsn tomid gegreyt.
Men hert do muzik fun Mozart derklingen,
di Zing-yinglekh Viener – zey zingen un zingen.
Der Straus mit sayn fidl fun gold unterm boym,
men geyt derkh'n shtotpark un meynt – s'iz a troym.
Alts iz do fridlekh, reynlekh un shtil.
Dos iz a leben, vi a yeder mentsh vil.
Men tantst un men freyt zikh, fargest gor di velt,
a yeder fargnigt zekh, nit shod far dos gelt!

Tsi kent ir a shtot nokh a zelkhe a sheyne,
mit platsn gor groise, mit geselekh kleyne,
vu gvirem in vayse palatsn fayn leben?
Di asilanten ober in finstre baraken dernebn
oyfs arbetsrekht yorn un yornlang varten,
un lebn togteglikh a tog gor an hartn.
„Mir zenen in Vien, der velt bester shtot!",
azoy trakhtn zey, vayl a hofenung men hot,
tsu geben a zukunft a gite far kinder.
Asil, asil ... Men vart oyf a vinder.

Tsi kent ir a shtot nokh a zelkhe a shtile,
Vu yidn kenen ruik zogn zeyr tfile?
Men treft zikh frimorgens tsum dav'nen in shil,
alts iz do ruik, beseder un shtil.
Men hot nisht ka moyre, men filt zikh do zikher,
vayl baym arayngong shteyt … a yiddisher bokher.
Es treft zikh afile, az es shteyt dort a meydl.
Zey shteyn nokhanand – es dreyt zikh dos reydl.
Zey shteyn far shabes un mitn der vokhen;
mit zeyr guf tsu zikhern dem yidns bitokhn.
Gegreyt tsu gebn zeyr leben oyfn ort …
A por politsyantn shteyn oykhet dort.
Dos ken ikh aykh zogn, tayere fraynt:
S'iz gor nit a shtile di shtilkeyt fun haynt.

Tsi kent ir a shtot nokh a zelkhe a fayne,
mit teaters, muzeyen un … mit vaser mit reynem?
Nor vos darf der viener hobn dos vaser?
Efsher tzum bodn, tsu zayn gor a naser?!
Der viener hot lib nit dos vaser, nor vayn.
Er zitst ba sayn „Heurigen" – do filt er zikh fayn.
Do ken er gefinen zayn fargenign –
dos fidl shpilt, skripet a lustikn nign.
Un shoyn zen'n fargesn tsores un zorgn,
der viener zingt zikh un trakht nisht fun morgn.
Er trakht nisht fun shnorers, vos leben in droysn,
leydendik noyt un hunger a groysn.
Menshen vos shlofn in park oyf a bank,
eylent un troyrik, fargesn un krank.
Vos geyt es mikh on, az zey frirn in frost? –
trakht er un lakht er un ruft freylekh: „Prost!"…

Tsi kent ir a shtot, vu men treft nokh fashisten,
men leynt in di tsaytungen fun neo-natsisten.
Der viener trakht zikh: „Alts naronim un yoldn!
S'iz shod far di tsayt", (un di tsayt iz dokh goldn).
„Vos darf ikh antkegn zey protestirn?
A kliger viener lost zikh nisht pushet farfirn!"
Azoy trakht er un vartendik kukt er zikh tsu,
vi andere brengen di zakhn tsu ru.
Vi andere geyn demonstritn oyf di gas,
bagegnen dem brenendn oyslender-has.
In zelkhe momentn kumt mir in mayn zin,
a lid, vos past take zeyr git far Vien:
„S'brent, brider, s'brent! Oyb di shtot iz aykh tayer,
shteyt nisht arum, lesht ineynem dos fayer!"…

Un dokh vil ikh zogn a interesante zakh.
Kh'hob do kritizirt, geshribn asakh,
dokh leb ikh in Vien. Az men freygt mikh, farvos,
kimt der entfer mir glaykh, un es shtelt zikh aroys,
az ikh hob lib di shtot, di hayzer, di gasn,
kh'hob lib do tsu lebn, khvil Vien nit farlasn.
Vien iz di shtot, vu es lebn mayne kinder,
Kh'hob zey zeyr lib, a yedn bazinder.
Vien iz di shtot, vu di fraynt mayne leben.
Tsi ken mir an andere shtot nokh mer gebn?

Dokh dos vikhtikste iz, az Vien iz di shtot,
vu a mentsh vi ikh take ale rekhtn hot.
A yid, vos gekimn fun Rusland amol,
hot dizelbign rekhtn, dem zelbign kol,
pinkt azoy vi a Viener, vos iz do geboyrn.
Un derfar leb ikh do, di hofenung nit farloyrn,
az alts vet nokh git, men vet lebn do in fridn,
muslimen und kristn un avade mir yidn.
Un di mentshn, vos hobn nit keyn eygenem gloybn,
veln oykhet dem sholem dankn un loybn.
Vayl nor, az der mentsh lebt mit andre in fridn,
kenen mir ale zayn take tsufridn.

Derfar, libe fraynt, baym tantzn gedenkn,
az andere mentshen vartn, hofn un benkn.
Oyf arbet, oyf hilf, oyf a shtikele broyt.
Fargest nit zeyr umet, fargest nit zeyr noyt.
Lomir zayn ale shtolz, az mir shtrekn zey di hant,
tzu leben in Vien in sholem mitanand.
Lomir ale zayn gliklekh un leben in freydn
in undzerer shtot, geefnet far yeydn.
Un s'vet kumen di tsayt, ikh zog vider un vider,
ale mentshn zenen glaykh. Ale zenen mir brider.

                                        Roman Grinberg

Jüdisches Museum Wien: David Rubinger und Ruth Corman präsentieren die deutsche Ausgabe des Buches „Israel durch mein Objektiv" (die Originalausgabe erschien 2007 unter dem Titel „Israel through my lens").
Jewish Museum Vienna: David Rubinger and Ruth Corman presenting the German edition "Israel durch mein Objektiv" of the book, that was first published in English as "Israel through my lens" in 2007.

Jüdisches Museum Wien, Museum Judenplatz: Eröffnung der Ausstellung „Jüdische Genies – Warhols Juden" mit Ronald Feldman von der Ronald Feldman Fine Arts Galerie in New York.
Jewish Museum Vienna, Museum Judenplatz: Exhibition opening: „Jewish Geniuses – Warhol's Jews" with Ronald Feldman from the Ronald Feldman Fine Arts gallery in New York.

Looshaus: Podiumsdiskussion über jüdische Identität unter der Moderation der Journalistin Susanne Scholl, mit Oberrabbiner Chaim Eisenberg, Hannah Lessing, Leiterin des Nationalfonds Österreich, und Musiker Edek Bartz.
Looshaus: panel discussion about Jewish Identity organized by the Jewish Museum Vienna and led by the journalist Susanne Scholl. Taking part in it are Chief Rabbi Chaim Eisenberg, Hannah Lessing, head of the National Restitution Fond, and the musician Edek Bartz.

Neueröffnung des Jüdischen Museums Wien
Reopening of the Jewish Museum Vienna

Der jüdische Kulturverein „Salon Vienna" organisiert das „World Café":
Diskussionsrunden zu verschiedenen Themen.
*The Jewish Cultural Club „Salon Vienna" organizes the „World Café":
discussion meetings about different topics.*

Opernsängerin Hilde Zadek (rechts)
Opera singer Hilde Zadek (right)

Der israelisch-österreichische Journalist und Schriftsteller Ari Rath
The Austrian-Israeli journalist and writer Ari Rath

David-Pauli Singer und Ari Rath bei der Enthüllung der Gedenktafel für Gotthold Antscherl, dem jüdischen Religionslehrer der Schubertschule, der mit vielen tausend österreichischen Juden in Mali Trostinec ermordet wurde.
David-Pauli Singer and Ari Rath at the revelation of the memorial plaque for Gotthold Antscherl, the Jewish teacher of religion at Schubert school, who was killed along with thousands of Austrian Jews in Maly Trostinec.

Wohin sind die schönen Tage verschwunden?
Wohin sind die schönen Tage unserer Kindheit in der Schubertschule verschwunden, unsere wunderbare Lehrerin Marie Blesson und die herrlichen Lieder, die wir dort lernen konnten. Warum wurde der Müllnertempel neben unserer Schule verbrannt und abgerissen, wo heute die Kinder der Schubertschule auf ihren Rädern fahren?

Maly Trostinec, was für ein fürchterlicher Name, den wir bisher nicht kannten, wo Tausende Menschen aus Österreich verbrannt und vergast wurden, nur weil sie Juden waren. Was für ein Wunder, dass wir diese grausamen Zeiten überleben konnten. Jetzt höre ich in meinen Gedanken die Melodie und die Wörter des Totenlieds, das wir vor 75 Jahren hier in diesem Haus gelernt haben:

Es ist ein Schnitter, der heißt Tod
Hat Gewalt vom großen Gott
Heut wetzt er sein Messer
Es schneid' schon viel besser
Bald wird er dreinschneiden
Wir müssen's nur leiden
Hüt Dich, schön's Blümelein

Ari Rath

Where have all the beautiful days gone?
Where have all the beautiful days of our childhood at Schubert school, our wonderful teacher Marie Blesson and the pretty songs that we learned there gone to?
Why was the Müllner temple next to our school where the children of today's Schubert school ride their bikes burnt and demolished?

Maly Trostinec, what a terrible name – of which we had no knowledge before – where thousands of people from Austria were burnt and gassed, just for being Jewish. What a miracle that we survived this cruel time. In my mind, I can now hear the melody and the words of lament that we have learnt in this house 75 years ago:

*There is a reaper man called Death,
who has power from the highest God
Today he is whetting his knife
this will give a fine cut
Soon he will be mowing
and we'll have to endure it
Beware, fair little flower*

Ari Rath

Theater Nestroyhof – Hamakom: Die israelische Autorin Zeruya Shalev liest aus ihrem neuen Buch „Für den Rest des Lebens".
Theater Nestroyhof – Hamakom: Israeli author Zeruya Shalev is reading from her new book "Für den Rest des Lebens".

Café Museum: Literaturabend mit Julya Rabinowich, die aus ihrer „Herznovelle" liest.
Café Museum: the Jewish writer Julya Rabinowich is reading from her new novel "Herznovelle".

Jüdisches Wien

Nachdem nun die Generation abgetreten ist, die sich noch gut an die 200.000 Juden in Wien erinnert hatte, nachdem nicht nur die Juden tot und weg waren, sondern jetzt auch ihre Peiniger tot und begraben, werden die toten Juden zu den guten Juden. Nicht nur jene damals, die unser Wien so eindrucksvoll prägten, nicht nur die Schnitzlers, Roths, Mahlers, auch die Opfer der Shoah – gute Juden, arme Juden.
Eine neue Generation von Wienerinnen/Wienern: Die können teils nicht verstehen, was man den Juden antat.
Und die Juden heute in Wien? Diese neue Generation? Zwar stammen die meisten nicht aus Wien, sondern ihre Eltern sind – wie auch schon einst – aus dem Osten gekommen oder zurück von Israel. Aber sie beleben diese Stadt. Sie sind selbstbewusst und tun schon so, als sei es selbstverständlich, als Jüdin/Jude in Wien zu leben und fröhlich zu leben.
Denn Wien ist heute eine gute Stadt. Ein guter Ort. Nicht für alle.
Die Stadt profitiert kräftig vom einstigen jüdischen Wien. Sie verdient. Fast so gut wie an Johann Strauß. Immer eindringlicher tritt den Heutigen ins Bewusstsein, was die Stadt einst verloren hat.

Kommt ein neues, reiches jüdisches Leben, eine Wiedergeburt? Ist das eine Falle?
Sind's in fünfzig Jahren wieder 200.000? Eine Gefahr für Wien? Eine neue Judenbelagerung? Oder werden wir angekommen sein und geblieben hundert Jahre und mehr? Weil aus Wien Makom geworden ist. Ein Lieblingsort. Eine Falle! Eine Falle?

Robert Schindel

Jewish Vienna

As the generation that could remember the 200,000 Jews in Vienna very well has now disappeared because not just the Jews are dead and gone, but also their tormentors are now dead and buried, the dead Jews finally become the good Jews. And not only those who back then impressively shaped our Vienna, not only those like Schnitzler, Roth, Mahler but also the victims of the Shoah – good Jews, poor Jews.
There is a new generation of Viennese: they cannot quite understand what had been done to the Jews.
And the Jews who live in Vienna today? This new generation? Most of them do not originate from Vienna but their parents came here – as once before – from Eastern Europe or returned from Israel.
But they enliven this city. They are self-confident and act as if it were natural for Jews to live in Vienna – to happily live in Vienna.
Because today's Vienna is a good city. A good place. Not for everyone, though.
The city strongly benefits from the former Jewish Vienna. It makes good money out of it. Almost as good as of Johann Strauss. We become more and more vividly aware of what the city once lost.

Will there be a new and rich Jewish life – a renaissance? Is it a trap? Will there be another 200,000 people in fifty years? A threat for Vienna? A new Jewish siege? Or will we have settled and persisted for a hundred years and more? Because Vienna has turned into Makom. A favourite place. A trap! A trap?

Robert Schindel

Schriftsteller Robert Schindel, Robert Menasse und Doron Rabinovici
Austrian writers Robert Schindel, Robert Menasse and Doron Rabinovici

Schriftsteller Vladimir Vertlib liest aus seinem Buch
„Schimons Schweigen".
*Author Vladimir Vertlib is reading from his novel
„Schimons Schweigen".*

Jüdisches Filmfestival Wien: Präsentation des Filmes „Wunderkind" mit Konstantin Wecker in der Urania, im Bild mit Festival-Direktor Frédéric-Gérard Kaczek
Vienna Jewish Film Festival: sneak preview of „Wunderkind" with Konstantin Wecker in the Urania; Festival director Frédéric-Gérard Kaczek

Künstlerhaus: Jewish Welcome Service hat die Künstlerin Alice Goldin aus Südafrika eingeladen und eine Ausstellung im Künstlerhaus anlässlich ihres 90. Geburtstages organisiert. Alice Goldin wurde 1922 in Wien geboren und emigrierte 1938 via England nach Südafrika.
Künstlerhaus: Jewish Welcome Service invited the South African artist Alice Goldin to Austria and organized an exhibition of her work at the Künstlerhaus. She was born in Vienna in 1922 and left in 1938 via England to South Africa.

Das Café Centropa findet einmal im Monat statt: Besonderer Gast Arik Brauer liest aus seiner Autobiografie und singt.
Café Centropa takes place once a month: special guest Arik Brauer is reading from his autobiography and singing some of his songs.

Oscar Bronner, Herausgeber der Tageszeitung „Der Standard", in seinem Büro
Oscar Bronner, chief editor of the daily newspaper „Der Standard", in his office

Die Fotografin Lisl Steiner: 1938 nach Argentinien emigriert und später in die USA
Photographer Lisl Steiner: emigrated in 1938 first to Argentina and later to the United States

Galerie Erich Lessing in der Weihburggasse 22: Der Magnum-Fotograf Erich Lessing arbeitet im Alter von 89 Jahren noch immer. Ein Porträt von Bruno Kreisky, als er Außenminister war.
Photogallery Lessingimages.com, Weihburggasse 22: The Magnum photographer Erich Lessing is still working at the age of 89. A portrait of the foreign minister Bruno Kreisky.

IKG Seitenstettengasse: „WINA-Magazin"-Chefredakteurin Julia Kaldori
Jewish Community Vienna, Seitenstettengasse: WINA magazine chief editor Julia Kaldori

Redaktionssitzung des Magazins „Nu": Peter Menasse, Danielle Spera, Barbara Tóth, Erwin Javor und Martin Engelberg
Editorial meeting "Nu" magazine: Peter Menasse, Danielle Spera, Barbara Tóth, Erwin Javor and Martin Engelberg

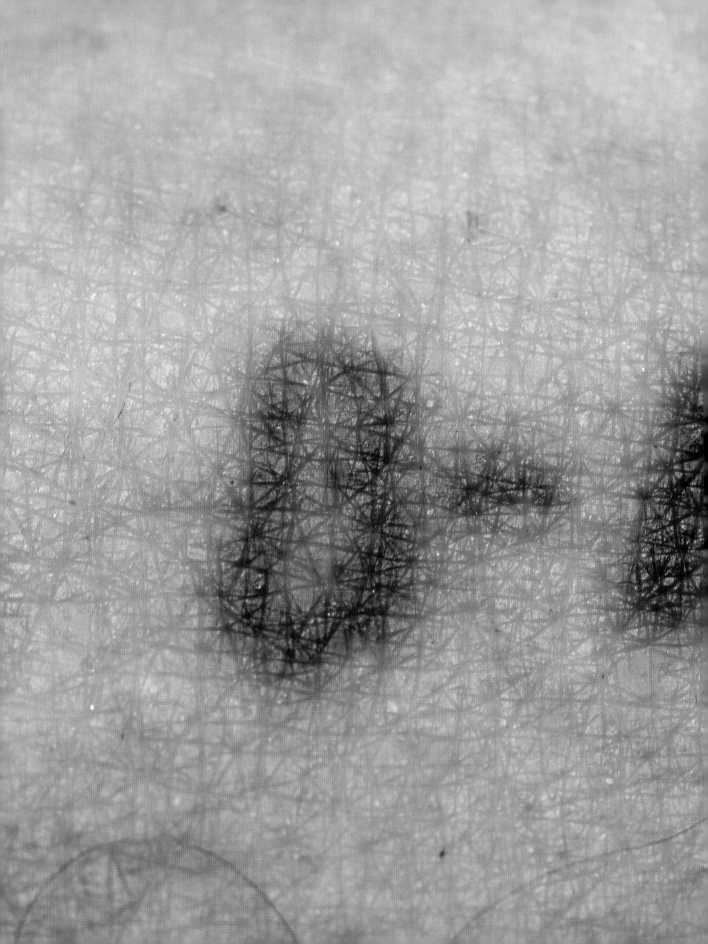

Walter Fantl-Brumlik, Holocaust-Überlebender.
Von diesem Familienporträt haben nur er und seine Tante überlebt.
Walter Fantl-Brumlik, Holocaust survivor. He and his aunt in the family portrait are the only survivors.

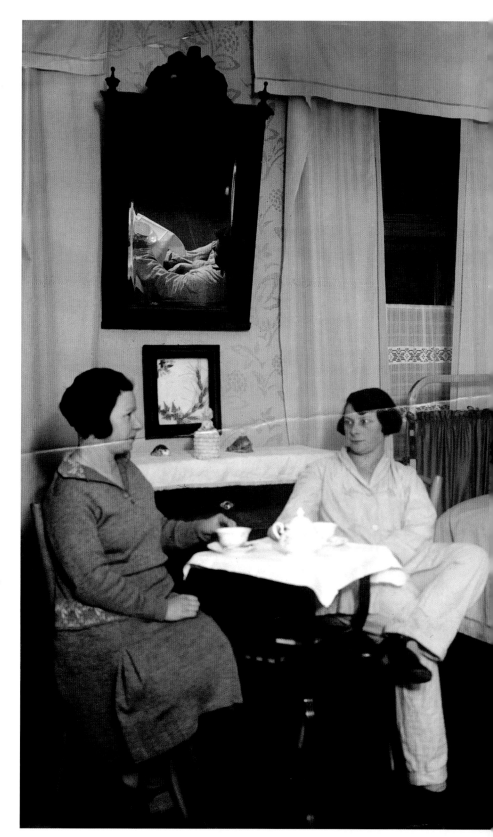

Henriette und Olga Medak in ihrer Wohnung in der Semperstraße 59 im 9. Wiener Gemeindebezirk. Foto vor 1929. Henriette wurde 1942 nach der Deportation aus Wien in Riga ermordet.
Henriette and Olga Medak in their apartment at Semperstrasse 59. The photo was taken before 1929. Henriette was deported and murdered in Riga in 1942.

Hansi Tausig besucht zum ersten Mal seit 1938 die Wohnung ihrer Tanten. Sie unterhält sich mit der heutigen Bewohnerin.
Hansi Tausig visits the apartment of her aunts the first time since 1938. She is talking with the present owner.

Da stand ich also

Da stand ich also vor dem Haus Nr. 59 in der Semperstraße. Hier haben meine Großeltern gewohnt, hier ist meine Mutter aufgewachsen, hier hat meine Tante Jetti gewohnt, bis sie 1938 von den Nazis in den Osten verschleppt und ermordet wurde. Die Wohnung wurde arisiert.

Es waren armselige Wohnungen, zwei nebeneinander, die erste Küche/Kabinett, die zweite Küche/Zimmer. Wasser und Toilette am Gang. Gemeinsam mit zwei weiteren Mietern. Ich habe immer wieder an diese Wohnung denken müssen, im Exil – ich konnte als Hausgehilfin nach England flüchten. In einer dieser winzigen Wohnungen haben meine Großeltern mit sieben Kindern gewohnt. Nie schliefen sie nur zu zweit in einem Bett. Erst als die älteren die Bürgerschule abgeschlossen hatten und zu Lehrlingen „herangewachsen" waren, schon ein bisschen eigenes Geld verdienten, wurde die Nebenwohnung gemietet. Tante Jetti, sie blieb unverheiratet, war für mich die „Gebildete", sprach Hochdeutsch. Die anderen Geschwister sprachen alle Wiener Dialekt. Ich erinnere mich sehr gut an sie, sie hat mein Interesse an Literatur geweckt.

Zurück zum Anfang: Ein Mann in mittleren Jahren, ein Fotograf, der wunderschöne, künstlerische Fotos macht, möchte im Bild festhalten, wie jüdische Wohnungen vor Hitlers Einmarsch ausgesehen haben – und wie sie nach den Arisierungen aussehen.

So hat er es zuwege gebracht, mit der jetzigen Mieterin der Wohnung meiner Familie Kontakt aufzunehmen. Sie ist nicht die Ariseurin, hat die Wohnung erst Jahrzehnte nach 1938 erworben. Sie ist eine ganz liebe Dame, eine Künstlerin, Malerin und Bildhauerin, aus Deutschland kommend, aber schon lange in Wien, und hat hier auch schon mehrmals ausgestellt.

Nun standen wir also vor dem Haustor – ich sage wir, weil meine Familie, Sohn, Schwiegertochter, Enkel, mitgekommen war. Sie hatten schon so viel von diesen beiden Wohnungen gehört. Sie waren neugierig – aufgeregt war nur ich.

Ich hatte zwar geahnt, dass es anders ausschauen würde, weil man ja weiß, dass diese alten Wohnungen total umgebaut werden, Kleinwohnungen zusammengezogen, die Toiletten, die Gänge etc. alles eingebaut. Aber so hatte ich es nicht erwartet. Ich konnte beim besten Willen nicht mit Sicherheit feststellen, wo früher gekocht, gesessen, geschlafen worden ist. Aber da die Außenwände und die Fenster unverändert bleiben mussten, war grad die Stelle, wo das alte Foto gemacht worden ist, unverändert.

Da saßen nun die Dame des Hauses und ich in der wunderschönen, mit Bildern und Skulpturen ausgestatteten Wohnung einander gegenüber, kleines Tischerl in der Mitte – wie auf dem alten Foto. Wenn das meine Großeltern oder die kunstsinnige Tante Jetti erlebt hätten.

Ich dankte es in diesen Minuten meinem Schicksal, dass es mir in meinem Alter nicht mehr möglich ist zu weinen – meine Tränendrüsen funktionieren nicht mehr. So konnte ich witzelnd meine Emotion kontrollieren. Ich kann mich ehrlich freuen, dass ein so netter Mensch ein so wunderschönes Heim hat. Tante Jetti hätte sich auch gefreut.

Hansi Tausig

Here I was

Here I was, standing in Semperstrasse in front of house number 59. This is where my grandparents used to live, where my mother grew up and where aunt Jetti lived until the Nazis abducted her into the East and murdered her in 1938. The apartment was Aryanized.

Once there were two adjoined and piteous apartments, the first comprising kitchen and closet, the second kitchen and bedroom. Water and toilet were in the hallway, shared with two other tenants. Over and over again, I was thinking about this apartment while I was in exile – I managed to escape to England where I worked as a housemaid. My grandparents lived in one of these apartments with their seven children. The two of them never had their bed just for themselves. It was not until the eldest children graduated from secondary school, became apprentices and earned some money on their own, that they could rent the adjacent apartment. To me, aunt Jetti, who never got married, was the educated person in our family – she spoke standard German. All the other siblings spoke Viennese dialect. I remember her very well; she aroused my interest in literature.

Back to the beginning: a middle-aged man, a photographer, who takes beautiful, artistic pictures, wants to capture on film how Jewish apartments looked before the German invasion – and how they looked after the Aryanization.

He managed to contact the current tenant of my family's apartment. She was not the one who Aryanized it, as she had bought the apartment decades after 1938. She is a lovely lady, an artist, a paintress and sculptress, who is from Germany, but has lived in Vienna for a long time and already staged here her own exhibitions for several times.

We were now standing in front of the entry door – I am saying we, because my family (my son, my daughter-in-law and my grandson) came along. They have heard so much about those two apartments, they were curious – I was the only one who was excited.

I have guessed that it would look different, as I knew that these old apartments have been completely rebuilt, transformed into small apartments, where toilets, hallways etc. are included. But I did not expect it to be like that. By no stretch of the imagination was I able to tell where we had cooked, eaten, slept back then. As the external wall and the windows had to be left unchanged, the only place that had stayed the same was where we had taken the old picture.

There I sat face to face with the lady of the house of this beautiful apartment that was decorated with pictures and sculptures, a small table between us – just as in the old picture.

If only my grandparents or my art-minded aunt Jetti could have seen this.

During those minutes I was grateful that, due to my age, I was no longer able to cry – my tear glands do not work anymore. I could therefore make jokes and control my emotions. I am honestly glad that such a nice person owns this wonderful home. Aunt Jetti would have been pleased, too.

Hansi Tausig

Tag des Gedenkens an die Opfer des Nationalsozialismus am 27. Jänner – Tag der Befreiung von Auschwitz
International Holocaust Remembrance Day, 27 January – the day Auschwitz was liberated

Frau mit israelischer Flagge im Weiheraum/Äußeres Burgtor
Woman with Israeli flag at Weiheraum/Äusseres Burgtor

Konzentrationslager Mauthausen, 8. Mai: Gedenkveranstaltung mit 7000 Menschen aus ganz Europa, Amerika, Kanada und Kuba. Überlebende führen den Umzug an – der Franzose Henri Ledroit (im khakifarbenen Anzug), rechts daneben der Österreicher Pepi Glatt und rechts von ihm der jüdisch-ungarische Professor Erno Lazarovits.
Concentration Camp Mauthausen, May 8th: commemorative service attended by about 7000 people from all over Europe, United States, Canada and Cuba. Survivors leading the march into the camp – French Henri Ledroit (Khaki colored suit) next to him on the right Austrian Pepi Glatt and right of him Jewish Hungarian Prof. Erno Lazarovits.

Jüdische Gedenkfeier in Mauthausen am 8. Mai, organisiert von der Wiener Kultusgemeinde – Ossi Deutsch hält eine Ansprache.
Jewish Memorial service in Mauthausen organized by the Jewish Community Vienna, May 8th – Ossi Deutsch is giving a speech.

Heldenplatz: Rechte Burschenschaften halten eine Wache am Grabmal des unbekannten Soldaten am 8. Mai.
Heldenplatz: Right wing fraternities holding a vigil next to the tomb of the unknown soldier on May 8th.

Demonstration gegen den Aufmarsch der rechten Burschenschafter am Heldenplatz. Im Bild Dr. Ariel Muzicant.
Demonstration against right wing fraternities at Heldenplatz.
Dr. Ariel Muzicant holding a speech.

Der Verein „Steine der Erinnerung": Vorsitzende Elisabeth Ben David-Hindler und der Überlebende Moritz Nagler eröffnen 4 Stationen der Erinnerung im 1. Bezirk.
The association "Stones of Rememberence": Chairwoman Elisabeth Ben David-Hindler and the survivor Moritz Nagler are opening up 4 stations of rememberence in the 1st district.

Stones of Remembrance

My grandparents, Leopold and Mathilde Feldstein were murdered in the Holocaust. Using the few letters from my grandfather and information found in various records, I had put together the facts around their deaths. They had lived at Werdertorgasse 17, but on 27 May 1938 Leopold was arrested. After being held in Dachau and Buchenwald he returned to Vienna on 23 April 1939. Despite having a visa to emigrate to Bolivia, Leopold was still in Vienna when the war began (a letter of 29 July mentions that his arm was broken and in a full cast) and on 26/27 October, he was deported to Nisko, Poland. From there he made his way to Lemburg, where he arrived on 11 November. The last existing letter from Leopold to his daughter in Switzerland is dated 16 June 1940. Just over a year later, Lemburg was taken by the German army and Leopold was murdered at some point after that. Mathilde Feldstein, my grandmother, remained at Werdertorgasse 17 until her transportation on 20 May 1942. Mathilde arrived at Male Trostinec on 26 May and was murdered.

In June 2010 I read an article on the Stolperstein project in Germany. I contacted them to ask if they placed their "stones" in Austria and was given details of Steine der Erinnerung. Now, just over a year later on 2 July 2011, I was standing in front of what had been my father's family home, next to a plaque commemorating my grandparents.

Trying to unravel all the emotions of that morning is difficult. I had already gone through feelings of anger at the manner of my grandparents' deaths. Instead, I came to the Werdertorgasse with a feeling of deep sadness. I was sad that I never had a chance to know my grandparents and that sadness is still with me. No matter how much more I discover about their lives, it will never be enough: knowledge is no substitute for experience and love. But there were good feelings too: I met people with similar stories and I have begun to understand that my father's unwillingness to talk in detail about the fate of his parents is not so unusual. I also felt what I can only describe as a "proud defiance". I stood there as a reminder to the ghosts of those who perpetrated the horror that engulfed so many millions that they failed: Leopold and Mathilde's family has now reached its fourth generation. And there was a feeling of satisfaction: the plaques were placed to remember my grandparents and to remind those who pass by of what happened.

Finally, there was, and is, a feeling of completeness. After more than 70 years, Leopold and Mathilde Feldstein have come home.

Richard Fenton, Edinburgh, Scotland

Steine der Erinnerung

Meine Großeltern Leopold und Mathilde Feldstein wurden im Holocaust getötet. Die Briefe meines Großvaters und die Informationen, die ich in verschiedenen Aufzeichnungen finden konnte, haben mir geholfen, die Fakten rund um ihren Tod zusammenzusetzen. Sie wohnten in der Werdertorgasse 17, doch am 27. Mai 1938 wurde Leopold verhaftet. Nachdem er in Dachau und Buchenwald festgehalten worden war, kehrte er am 23. April 1939 nach Wien zurück. Obwohl er ein Visum besaß, mit dem er nach Bolivien emigrieren hätte können, war Leopold noch immer in Wien, als der Krieg begann (in einem Brief vom 29. Juli schrieb er, dass er sich den Arm gebrochen hatte und einen Gips tragen musste), und am 26./27. Oktober wurde er nach Nisko in Polen deportiert. Von dort konnte er sich am 11. November nach Lemberg durchschlagen. Der letzte vorhandene Brief von Leopold an seine in der Schweiz lebende Tochter ist mit 16. Juni 1940 datiert. Nur ein Jahr später wurde Lemberg von der deutschen Armee eingenommen und Leopold getötet. Meine Großmutter Mathilde Feldstein blieb bis zu ihrer Deportation am 20. Mai 1942 in der Werdertorgasse 17. Sie kam am 26. Mai in Maly Trostinec an, wo sie getötet wurde.

Im Juni 2010 las ich einen Artikel über das deutsche Projekt Stolperstein. Ich kontaktierte die Verantwortlichen, fragte, ob sie ihre Steine auch in Österreich setzen würden, und erhielt daraufhin nähere Informationen über die Steine der Erinnerung. Am 2. Juli 2011 – etwas mehr als ein Jahr später – stand ich vor dem Haus, das einst der Familie meines Vaters gehörte, vor einer Gedenktafel, die an meine Großeltern erinnerte.

Es fällt mir schwer, die Gefühle, die ich an diesem Morgen verspürte, zu beschreiben. Die Art und Weise, wie meine Großeltern gestorben waren, hatte mich sehr wütend gemacht. Doch die Werdertorgasse betrat ich mit einem Gefühl der tiefen Traurigkeit. Es stimmte mich traurig, dass ich niemals die Gelegenheit bekommen würde, meine Großeltern kennenzulernen, und diese Traurigkeit empfinde ich immer noch. So viel ich auch über ihr Leben erfahre, es wird nie genug sein – Wissen ist kein Ersatz für Erfahrung und Liebe. Doch ich erfuhr auch viel Schönes: Ich traf Menschen mit ähnlichen Geschichten und begann zu begreifen, dass der Widerwille, den mein Vater verspürt hatte, wenn er mehr über das Schicksal seiner Eltern erzählen sollte, nicht ungewöhnlich ist. Ich fühlte auch etwas, das ich am besten als „stolzen Trotz" beschreiben kann. Ich stand hier als Erinnerung an die Geister jener, die diese Verbrechen verübt hatten, und an die Tatsache, dass sie gescheitert waren: Die Familie von Leopold und Mathilde besteht jetzt schon in der vierten Generation. Ich empfand auch ein Gefühl der Zufriedenheit. Die Tafeln wurden errichtet, um meiner Großeltern zu gedenken und um all jene, die daran vorbeigehen, an das Geschehene zu erinnern.

Endlich spürte ich ein Gefühl der Abgeschlossenheit, das immer noch anhält. Nach mehr als 70 Jahren sind Leopold und Mathilde Feldstein endlich nach Hause zurückgekehrt.

Richard Fenton, Edinburgh, Schottland

„Mahnmal für die österreichischen jüdischen Opfer der Shoa" der englischen Künstlerin Rachel Whiteread am Judenplatz
The Judenplatz Holocaust Memorial by the English artist Rachel Whiteread stands for the Austrian Jewish victims of the Shoah

Jewish Welcome Service Vienna: bei einem Besuch im Bundeskanzleramt, Führung von Dr. Manfred Matzka
Jewish Welcome Service: organized a visit to the Federal Chancellery and was given a tour by Dr. Manfred Matzka

Feste Feasts

Seiten 134/135: Jugendgruppe Hillel bei der Purimfeier
Pages 134/135: Youth group Hillel having a Purim celebration

Purimfest der Organisation Chabad in der Lauder Business School
Purim party organized by the organization Chabad at the Lauder Business School

Purimfest der Jugendbewegung Hashomer Hatzair
Purim party organized by the Youth Movement Hashomer Hatzair

S-Club: Purim Balagan. Purimparty für Studenten und junge Erwachsene
S-Club: Purim Balagan. Purim party for students and young adults

Jüdische Österreichische HochschülerInnen (JÖH): Sederabend mit jüdischen Studenten in Wien
Jewish Austrian Students: Pesach seder for Jewish students in Vienna

Sederabend bei der Jugendorganisation Hashomer Hatzair
Seder at the youth organization Hashomer Hatzair

Chabad organisiert im Bet Halevi in der Woche vor Pessach ein Matze-Backen für jüdische Schüler aus Wiener Schulen.
Beit Halevi a Chabad owned house is doing matzah baking for Jewish school children in Vienna in the week before Pesach.

Chabad Haus Beit Halevi: Matze-Backen für jüdische Schulkinder aus den verschiedenen Wiener Schulen in der Woche vor Pessach.
Beit Halevi a Chabad owned house is doing matzah baking for Jewish school children in Vienna in the week before Pesach.

Matze-Backen in der Lilienbrunngasse vor dem Beginn des Pessach-Festes
Matzah baking at Lilienbrunngasse before Pesach starts

Große Mohrengasse: Kinder waschen Geschirr in der Mikwe vor dem Beginn des Pessach-Festes.
Grosse Mohrengasse: boys wash family dishes in the Mikveh before Pesach.

Hashomer Hatzair: Lag baOmer-Feier an der Neuen Donau
Hashomer Hatzair: Lag BaOmer celebration at the Camping ground Neue Donau

ZPC-Schule: Lag baOmer-Feier, organisiert von Jad Bejad und Club Chai
ZPC School: Lag baOmer celebration organized by Jad Bejad and Club Chai

Lag baOmer: Chabad-Feier für Studenten der Lauder Business School
Lag baOmer: celebration organized by Chabad for students of the Lauder Business School

Jom Ha'atzmaut (Tag der Unabhängigkeit – Feier der israelischen Unabhängigkeit 1948)
Club Night, organisiert von der Israelitischen Kultusgemeinde Wien
Yom Ha'atzmaut (commemorates Israel's declaration of Independence in 1948)
Club Night organized by the Jewish Community Vienna

ZPC Schule: Lag baOmer, organisiert von Jad Bejad and Club Chai.
Der Präsident der Israelitischen Kultusgemeinde, Oskar Deutsch, und seine Söhne spielen Tischtennis mit Vize-Präsident Chanan Babacsayv.
ZPC Schule: Lag baOmer organized by Jad Bejad and Club Chai.
President of the Jewish Community Oskar Deutsch and his sons play table tennis with the vice-president Chanan Babacsayv.

Straßenfest am Judenplatz, Makkabiade 2011: Die Makkabi-Fackel wird nach dem Lauf durch das Wiener Zentrum zum Judenplatz gebracht.
Jewish Street Festival, Maccabi Games 2011: Maccabi torch is carried to Judenplatz, after a run through the center of Vienna

Straßenfest am Judenplatz
Jewish Street Festival, Judenplatz

Sukkot (Laubhüttenfest): Chabad-Rabbiner Zalman Raskin mit Palmzweig (hebr. Lulav) und Etrog (Zitronatzitrone)
Sukkot: Chabad-Rabbi Zalman Raskin with Lulav and Etrog

Chabad-Rabbiner Zalman Raskin gibt eine Unterweisung für Sukkot.
Chabad Rabbi Zalman Raskin is giving instructions for Sukkot.

Stadttempel: Oberrabbiner Paul Chaim Eisenberg erzählt von Sukkot in der Sukka (Laubhütte).
Central City Temple: Chief Rabbi Paul Chaim Eisenberg talking about Sukkot in the Sukkah.

Stadttempel: Rabbiner Schlomo Hofmeister entzündet Öllampen in der Sukka.
Central City Temple: Rabbi Schlomo Hofmeister is lighting oil lamps in the Sukkah.

Lauder Business School: Simchat-Torah-Feier in der Ohel Abraham Synagoge
Lauder Business School: celebration of Simchat Torah at Ohel Avram Synagogue

Chanukka-Feier im Jüdischen Museum Wien
Hanukkah celebration at the Jewish Museum in Vienna

Chanukka-Feier für die Studenten der Lauder Business School, organisiert von Chabad. Die Feier fand auf dem Eislaufplatz Engelmann im 17. Bezirk statt.
Hanukkah celebration, organized by Chabad, for the students of the Lauder Business School. The celebration took place at the ice skating rink Engelmann in the 17th district of Vienna.

Chanukka-Feier am Stephansplatz in der Wiener Innenstadt
Hanukkah celebration in the center of Vienna at St. Stephen's Square

Private Chanukka-Feier
Private Hanukkah celebration

Jüdisches Museum Wien, Or-Sarua-Synagoge: die Überreste der ältesten Synagoge der Stadt aus dem 15. Jahrhundert. Die erste Chanukka-Kerze wird hier von der Misrachi-Gemeinde entzündet.
Jewish Museum Vienna: Or Sarua Synagogue are the remains of the oldest synagogue in the city date to the 15th century. The first Hanukkah candle is lit by the Misrachi community in this location.

Chanukka-Feier bei Rabbiner Hofmeister
Hanukkah celebration at Rabbi Hofmeister's apartment

Mit freundlicher Unterstützung von:

Für Renata Rainer, Ira Wunder (my mentors)

ISBN 978-3-99300-099-8 (Buch)
ISBN 978-3-99300-105-6 (Katalog)
© 2012 Metroverlag
Verlagsbüro W. GmbH
info@metroverlag.at
Alle Rechte vorbehalten
Printed in the EU